Becoming a Millionaire with AI: Transforming Ideas into Wealth

Table of Contents

Introduction

Brief Overview of AI

Artificial Intelligence (AI) is a transformative technology that mimics human intelligence, enabling machines to perform tasks that typically require human cognition. From its inception to the present, AI has become an integral part of modern business, driving efficiency, innovation, and competitive advantage.

Key Milestones in AI Development

Development of the First AI Program, Logic Theorist, in 1955

The Logic Theorist, developed by Allen Newell and Herbert A. Simon, in 1955, marked the birth of AI. This program was designed to mimic human problem-solving skills and proved mathematical theorems. It introduced the concept of heuristic problem-solving, which involves using practical methods to find solutions when an optimal solution is challenging to identify. The Logic Theorist's ability to prove 38 of the first 52 theorems in Whitehead and Russell's "Principia Mathematica" signalled a significant breakthrough in computer science and cognitive psychology.

IBM's Deep Blue Defeating Chess Champion Garry Kasparov in 1997

In 1997, IBM's Deep Blue, a chess-playing computer, defeated world chess champion Garry Kasparov. This event showcased AI's potential in strategic thinking and complex problem-solving. Profound Blue's victory resulted from sophisticated algorithms capable of evaluating millions of chess positions per second. The machine's ability to assess various strategies and adapt its play based on Kasparov's moves demonstrated AI's capacity to handle complex, real-time decision-making tasks, underscoring the potential for AI in other strategic domains.

Google's AlphaGo Beating Go Champion Lee Sedol in 2016

AlphaGo, developed by DeepMind, a subsidiary of Google, defeated Go champion Lee Sedol in 2016. Go, a game known for its complexity and intuition-based strategy, highlighted AI's advanced pattern recognition and decision-making capabilities. AlphaGo's success was powered by deep neural networks and reinforcement learning, enabling it to evaluate vast numbers of potential moves and learn from previous games. This milestone illustrated AI's ability to tackle tasks requiring intuition and creativity, opening new possibilities for AI applications in medical diagnosis, financial forecasting, and autonomous driving.

Types of AI

Narrow AI: Specialized in One Task

Narrow AI, also known as weak AI, is designed to perform a specific task, such as facial recognition, language translation, or playing chess. It excels in its designated function but cannot generalise its skills to other tasks. Narrow AI systems are prevalent in various applications today, including virtual assistants like Siri and Alexa, recommendation systems on platforms like Netflix and Amazon, and fraud detection in banking.

General AI: Ability to Perform Any Intellectual Task

General AI, or strong AI, can understand, learn, and apply knowledge across various tasks, similar to human intelligence. General AI can perform any intellectual task that a human can, with the flexibility to switch between tasks and learn new ones without human intervention. While still theoretical, achieving General AI represents the ultimate goal for AI researchers, as it would mark the creation of machines capable of independent reasoning and problem-solving in any context.

Superintelligence: Surpassing Human Intelligence

Superintelligence refers to AI that surpasses human intelligence, potentially outperforming humans in virtually every field. This concept raises important ethical and safety considerations, as superintelligent AI could profoundly impact society, the economy, and human existence. Theoretical discussions about superintelligence often concern ensuring that such robust AI systems are aligned with human values and goals, preventing unintended consequences.

Importance of AI in Modern Business

Enhancing Efficiency and Productivity

AI technologies automate routine tasks, optimise operations, and enhance decision-making processes, increasing business efficiency and productivity. For example, AI-powered chatbots handle customer service inquiries, reducing the workload for human agents. AI-driven predictive maintenance ensures machinery operates smoothly in manufacturing, minimising downtime and extending equipment lifespan. AI also helps streamline supply chain operations, optimise inventory levels, and reduce operational costs.

Driving Innovation and Competitive Advantage

AI fosters innovation by enabling the development of new products, services, and business models, giving companies a competitive edge in the market. AI algorithms analyse vast data to uncover insights that inform product development and marketing strategies. For instance, AI in healthcare can accelerate drug discovery by predicting molecular behaviour, while AI-driven algorithms can optimise investment portfolios in finance. Businesses that leverage AI effectively can innovate faster and adapt quickly to changing market conditions.

Real-World Examples of AI Applications in Business

Businesses across various industries are leveraging AI to drive success. Predictive analytics help institutions detect fraudulent transactions and assess credit risks in finance. Retailers use AI for personalised marketing strategies, enhancing customer engagement and loyalty through tailored recommendations. In logistics, AI optimises delivery route planning, reducing fuel consumption and improving delivery times. These applications demonstrate AI's potential to revolutionise business operations, providing significant competitive advantages and driving growth.

Chapter 1: Understanding AI

Basics of AI

Core Concepts

Artificial Intelligence (AI) involves simulating human intelligence processes by machines, particularly computer systems. These processes include learning (acquiring information and rules for using the information), reasoning (using rules to reach approximate or definite conclusions), and self-correction.

Algorithms

Algorithms are the backbone of AI, providing step-by-step instructions for machines to process data and make decisions. They enable AI systems to learn from and adapt to new information. Algorithms can range from simple if-then statements to complex mathematical models.

Neural Networks

Neural networks are computational models inspired by the human brain. They consist of interconnected nodes (neurons) that process data and learn patterns. Neural networks are fundamental to deep learning, a subset of AI, and are used to perform tasks such as image and speech recognition.

Data Processing

AI systems rely on vast data to learn and make informed decisions. Effective data processing techniques are essential for extracting valuable insights from raw data. This includes data cleaning, normalisation, and transformation processes.

Key Terms

Machine Learning

Machine learning is a subset of AI that enables systems to learn from data, identify patterns, and make decisions with minimal human intervention. It encompasses various techniques, including supervised, unsupervised, and reinforcement learning.

Deep Learning

Deep learning is a specialised form of machine learning that uses neural networks with many layers (deep neural networks) to analyse complex data patterns. It is particularly effective in image and speech recognition, natural language processing, and autonomous driving tasks.

Neural Networks

Neural networks are designed to recognise patterns and classify data like the human brain. They are used in deep learning to enable advanced AI capabilities. Neural networks can have multiple layers, including input, hidden, and output layers, each contributing to the learning process.

Machine Learning and Deep Learning

Overview of Machine Learning

Supervised Learning

Supervised learning involves training an AI model on labelled data where the desired output is known. The model learns to predict the output based on input data. Typical applications include spam detection, image classification, and predictive analytics.

Unsupervised Learning

Unsupervised learning deals with unlabeled data, where the AI system must find patterns and relationships without prior guidance on the desired outcomes. This technique is used for clustering, anomaly detection, and association tasks.

Reinforcement Learning

Reinforcement learning involves training AI models through trial and error. In this method, models learn to make decisions by receiving rewards or penalties based on their actions. This method is commonly used in robotics, game-playing, and self-driving cars.

Introduction to Deep Learning

Deep learning leverages deep neural networks to process and analyse large datasets. It excels in tasks requiring pattern recognition, such as image and speech recognition. Deep learning models can automatically extract features from raw data, reducing the need for manual feature engineering.

Applications and Real-World Examples

AI and machine learning applications span various industries, demonstrating their transformative potential:

- Healthcare: AI aids in diagnosing diseases, predicting patient outcomes, and personalising treatment plans.
- Finance: AI helps in fraud detection, risk management, and algorithmic trading.
- Marketing: AI enhances customer insights, automates customer service, and optimises marketing strategies.
- Manufacturing: AI improves quality control, predictive maintenance, and supply chain optimisation.
- Education: AI tailors educational content, automates administrative tasks, and generates educational materials.

These real-world examples highlight how AI technologies drive innovation and efficiency across different sectors.

By understanding the basics of AI, machine learning, and deep learning, as well as their applications, businesses can better appreciate the potential of these technologies to transform their operations and create new opportunities for growth and success.

Chapter 2: AI in Healthcare

Diagnostic Tools

Ai-driven imaging and Diagnostic Systems

AI-powered imaging systems have revolutionised the accuracy and speed of medical diagnoses by analysing medical images such as X-rays, MRIs, and CT scans. These systems use deep learning algorithms to detect anomalies and diseases, assisting radiologists in making more accurate and faster diagnoses. For example, AI can identify early signs of cancer in mammograms that the human eye might miss.

Case Studies in Radiology and Pathology

Numerous case studies highlight the effectiveness of AI in radiology and pathology. One notable example is the use of AI in detecting lung nodules in chest X-rays, significantly improving the early detection of lung cancer. Another case involves AI systems in pathology that analyse tissue samples to identify cancerous cells with high precision, thereby aiding pathologists in making more accurate diagnoses.

Personalised Treatment

AI for Personalized Medicine and Treatment Plans

AI enables the development of personalised medicine by analysing a patient's genetic, environmental, and lifestyle data. This comprehensive analysis allows individualised treatment plans tailored to each patient's unique profile, improving treatment outcomes and patient satisfaction. For instance, AI can predict how a patient might respond to a particular medication, allowing doctors to select the most effective treatment with fewer side effects.

Examples in Oncology and Genomics

In oncology, AI aids oncologists in developing personalised cancer treatment plans based on a patient's genetic makeup and the molecular characteristics of their tumour. This approach, known as precision oncology, has led to more effective and targeted cancer therapies. In genomics, AI helps identify genetic mutations associated with various diseases, enabling early intervention and personalised treatment strategies.

Case Studies of Personalized Treatment

Several case studies showcase the success of AI-driven personalised treatment plans. For example, in cancer treatment, AI has been used to analyse genetic data from patients with melanoma, leading to tailored immunotherapy treatments that significantly improve patient outcomes. Similarly, AI has been employed in cardiology to create individualised treatment plans for patients with heart disease, resulting in better management and prevention strategies.

Administrative Automation

AI for Streamlining Administrative Tasks

AI automates various administrative tasks in healthcare, such as appointment scheduling, billing, and record-keeping. This reduces the administrative burden on healthcare providers, allowing them to focus more on patient care. AI systems can handle repetitive tasks more efficiently and accurately, increasing operational efficiency and cost savings.

Examples of Healthcare Institutions

Healthcare institutions have successfully implemented AI-driven administrative automation. For instance, AI-powered chatbots handle patient inquiries and appointment scheduling, significantly reducing wait times and improving patient satisfaction. Automated billing systems use AI to process insurance claims and manage patient payments more efficiently, reducing errors and administrative costs.

Future Trends in AI Healthcare

The future of AI in healthcare is promising, with advancements expected in several areas:

1. AI-Driven Drug Discovery: AI is set to accelerate drug discovery processes by predicting how different compounds interact with biological targets, potentially reducing the time and cost required to develop new medications.

2. Robotic Surgery: AI-powered robotic systems are becoming more sophisticated, allowing for more precise and minimally invasive surgical procedures. These systems can assist surgeons in complex operations, improving patient outcomes and reducing recovery times.

3. Enhanced Telemedicine: AI will enhance telemedicine by providing real-time data analysis and decision support, enabling remote diagnosis and treatment. This will expand access to healthcare services, particularly in underserved areas.

4. Virtual Health Assistants: AI-driven virtual health assistants will become more prevalent. They will provide patients with personalised health advice, medication reminders, and lifestyle recommendations, thus improving overall health management.

5. Predictive Analytics for Preventive Care: AI will enable predictive analytics that identify patients at risk of developing certain conditions, allowing for early intervention and preventive care strategies.

In conclusion, AI is transforming healthcare by improving diagnostic accuracy, personalising treatment plans, automating administrative tasks, and driving future innovations. These advancements promise to enhance patient care, reduce costs, and increase the overall efficiency of healthcare systems.

Chapter 3: AI in Finance

Fraud Detection

How AI Identifies and Prevents Fraudulent Activities

AI uses sophisticated anomaly detection and predictive modelling techniques to identify suspicious transactions and prevent fraud. By continuously analysing transaction data, AI systems can detect patterns that deviate from the norm and flag them for further investigation. These systems learn from historical data to improve accuracy, adapt to new fraud tactics and reduce false positives.

Techniques: Anomaly Detection and Predictive Modeling

Anomaly detection involves identifying deviations from typical behaviour, which can indicate fraudulent activities. AI models can scan vast amounts of real-time transaction data, identifying outliers warranting further scrutiny. Predictive modelling uses historical data to forecast potential fraudulent activities. These models can predict fraud's likelihood by analysing transaction size, frequency, and location.

Case Studies in Fraud Detection

Several financial institutions have successfully implemented AI-based fraud detection systems. For instance, PayPal uses AI to analyse millions of daily transactions, accurately identifying fraudulent activities. Similarly, JP Morgan Chase employs AI to monitor transactions and detect anomalies, significantly reducing fraud-related losses. These case studies demonstrate how AI enhances the security and reliability of financial systems.

Algorithmic Trading

Role of AI in High-Frequency Trading

AI plays a crucial role in high-frequency trading (HFT) by analysing market data and executing trades at lightning speed. HFT algorithms use AI to identify market inefficiencies and capitalise on small price movements within milliseconds. This rapid execution and analysis enable traders to gain a competitive edge in the financial markets.

Benefits and Risks of AI in Algorithmic Trading

AI-driven algorithmic trading offers several benefits, including increased trading efficiency, reduced human error, and the ability to quickly process vast amounts of data. However, it also poses risks, such as market volatility and the potential for systemic failures due to algorithmic errors. Ensuring robust risk management and regulatory compliance is essential to mitigate these risks.

Case Studies in Algorithmic Trading

AI-driven trading strategies have demonstrated significant financial gains. For example, Renaissance Technologies, a hedge fund known for using AI in trading, has consistently outperformed the market. Another example is Goldman Sachs, which utilises AI algorithms to optimise its trading strategies, resulting in improved trading performance and profitability.

Personal Finance Management

AI-Powered Tools for Budgeting, Investment, and Financial Planning

AI-powered tools assist individuals in managing their finances by providing personalised budgeting, investment, and financial planning advice. To offer tailored recommendations, these tools analyse users' financial data, such as income, expenses, and investment portfolios. AI can help users set financial goals, track spending, and optimise their investments.

Case Studies in Personal Finance Management

AI-driven personal finance apps like Mint and YNAB (You Need A Budget) have helped millions of users improve their financial health. These apps use AI to categorise expenses, identify savings opportunities, and provide real-time financial insights. Robo-advisors like Betterment and Wealthfront use AI to create and manage investment portfolios, offering personalised investment strategies based on individual risk tolerance and financial goals.

Future Trends in AI Finance

The future of AI in finance promises several exciting advancements:

1. Robo-Advisors: The next generation of robo-advisors will offer even more sophisticated investment strategies, leveraging AI to optimise portfolios in real time and provide personalised financial advice.
2. Blockchain Integration: AI and blockchain technology will converge to enhance financial transactions' security, transparency, and efficiency. AI-driven analytics will benefit intelligent contracts and decentralised finance (DeFi) platforms.
3. Enhanced Risk Management: AI will play a vital role in risk management, using predictive analytics to anticipate market trends and potential risks. Financial institutions will leverage AI to enhance their compliance and regulatory frameworks.
4. AI-Driven Financial Products: Innovative financial products like AI-powered insurance policies and credit scoring systems will emerge. These products will offer more accurate risk assessments and tailored financial solutions.

In conclusion, AI is transforming the finance industry by enhancing fraud detection, optimising trading strategies, and improving personal finance management. As AI technology continues to evolve, it will drive further innovation and efficiency in the financial sector, offering new opportunities for growth and success.

Chapter 4: AI in Marketing

Customer Insights

AI for Analyzing Consumer Behavior and Preferences

AI revolutionises how businesses analyse consumer behaviour and preferences by processing vast amounts of data from multiple sources, such as social media, purchase history, and browsing patterns. Advanced AI algorithms identify trends, patterns, and correlations in this data, offering deep insights into customer needs and preferences. This enables businesses to create more personalised and effective marketing strategies.

Tools and Techniques for Customer Insights

Sentiment analysis, predictive analytics, and customer segmentation help businesses better understand their audience. Sentiment analysis uses natural language processing to determine the emotions behind customer reviews and social media posts. Predictive analytics forecasts future customer behaviours based on historical data, while customer segmentation divides the market into distinct groups based on demographics, behaviour, and other factors.

Case Studies in Customer Insights

Numerous businesses have leveraged AI-driven customer insights to enhance their marketing strategies. For example, Netflix uses AI to analyse viewing habits and recommend content tailored to individual preferences, resulting in higher engagement and customer satisfaction. Similarly, Starbucks uses predictive analytics to personalise marketing messages and offers based on customer purchase history and preferences, driving increased sales and loyalty.

Automated Customer Service

Chatbots and Virtual Assistants in Customer Support

AI-powered chatbots and virtual assistants provide instant customer support, efficiently handling queries and resolving issues. These systems use natural language processing to understand and respond to customer inquiries, offering 24/7 support and reducing the workload on human customer service agents.

Benefits of AI in Customer Service

AI enhances customer service by providing instant, accurate, and consistent responses. This leads to faster resolution times, higher customer satisfaction, and lower operational costs. AI systems can simultaneously handle many inquiries, ensuring no customer is left waiting.

Case Studies in Automated Customer Service

Companies like H&M and Sephora have successfully implemented AI-driven customer service solutions. H&M uses chatbots to assist customers with product searches, order tracking, and returns, improving customer satisfaction and operational efficiency. Sephora's virtual assistant provides personalised beauty advice and product recommendations, enhancing the shopping experience and increasing sales.

Marketing Optimization

AI for Optimizing Marketing Campaigns and Strategies

AI optimises marketing campaigns by analysing data to provide insights into campaign performance, audience targeting, and content effectiveness. AI can determine the best times to post on social media, suggest content topics, and identify the most effective advertising channels, ensuring that marketing efforts yield the highest return on investment.

Critical Applications of AI in Marketing Optimization

Critical applications include programmatic advertising, which uses AI to automate the buying and placement of ads in real-time, and personalised content delivery, which tailors marketing messages to individual users based on their behaviour and preferences. Predictive analytics can forecast campaign outcomes and optimise future marketing strategies.

Case Studies in Marketing Optimization

Companies like Coca-Cola and Nike have used AI to optimise their marketing efforts. Coca-Cola employs AI to analyse social media data and consumer feedback, helping to refine its marketing campaigns and product offerings. Nike uses AI-driven analytics to personalise marketing messages and offers, increasing engagement and conversion rates.

Future Trends in AI Marketing

Augmented Reality (AR) and AI Integration

The integration of AI and augmented reality (AR) is set to transform marketing by offering immersive and interactive customer experiences. AR applications, powered by AI, can provide virtual try-ons for fashion and beauty products or visualise home decor items in a customer's space.

Voice Search Optimization

With the growing use of voice-activated assistants like Siri, Alexa, and Google Assistant, optimising for voice search is becoming increasingly important. AI can help businesses adapt their content and SEO strategies to cater to voice search queries, ensuring they remain visible and accessible to customers.

Hyper-Personalized Marketing

AI will drive hyper-personalized marketing, where every customer interaction is tailored to individual preferences and behaviours. Advanced data analytics and machine learning algorithms will enable businesses to deliver highly relevant content, offers, and recommendations, significantly enhancing customer engagement and loyalty.

In conclusion, AI transforms marketing by providing deeper customer insights, automating customer service, and optimising marketing strategies. AI technology will unlock new opportunities for businesses to engage with their customers meaningfully and effectively, driving growth and competitive advantage.

Chapter 5: AI in Manufacturing

Smart Factories

Concept of Industry 4.0 and AI Integration

Industry 4.0 represents the fourth industrial revolution, integrating AI, IoT, and advanced robotics in manufacturing. This shift towards intelligent factories enables enhanced automation, real-time data analytics, and improved decision-making processes. AI systems monitor and optimise production lines, ensuring factories operate more efficiently and effectively.

Examples of intelligent Manufacturing AI-driven Systems

AI-driven manufacturing systems include autonomous robots, which can work alongside human workers to perform complex tasks precisely and consistently. AI also powers intelligent supply chain management systems, optimising logistics, inventory levels, and procurement processes. Predictive maintenance systems, another critical application, analyse equipment data to anticipate failures and schedule timely repairs, reducing downtime and maintenance costs.

Predictive Maintenance

AI for Predicting Equipment Failures and Maintenance Needs

Predictive maintenance uses AI to predict equipment failures before they occur, allowing for proactive maintenance scheduling. AI systems identify patterns and anomalies that indicate potential issues by analysing data from sensors embedded in machinery, enabling timely intervention.

Techniques for AI-Based Predictive Maintenance

Techniques for AI-based predictive maintenance include machine learning models, which learn from historical data to predict future failures, and anomaly detection, which identifies deviations from normal operating conditions. Predictive analytics also plays a crucial role, using statistical models to forecast maintenance needs based on equipment usage and condition.

Benefits of Predictive Maintenance

Predictive maintenance offers several benefits, including reduced downtime, extended equipment lifespan, and lower maintenance costs. It also enhances safety by preventing catastrophic failures and improves overall operational efficiency.

Case Studies in Predictive Maintenance

Several manufacturing companies have successfully implemented AI-driven predictive maintenance. For example, General Electric uses AI to monitor its jet engines and wind turbines, predicting maintenance needs and optimising performance. Siemens employs similar technology in its manufacturing plants, reducing equipment downtime and maintenance expenses.

Quality Control

AI for Real-Time Monitoring and Quality Assurance

AI enhances quality control by monitoring production processes in real-time and ensuring that products meet quality standards. AI systems use sensors and cameras to inspect products for defects, identify deviations from specifications, and ensure consistency.

Techniques for AI-Based Quality Control

Techniques for AI-based quality control include image recognition, which uses machine learning algorithms to analyse visual data and detect defects, and statistical process control, which monitors production metrics to identify and correct deviations. AI systems can also use predictive analytics to forecast quality issues and implement preventive measures.

Benefits of AI in Quality Control

AI-driven quality control improves product quality, reduces waste, and enhances customer satisfaction. By identifying defects early in production, AI helps manufacturers maintain high standards and avoid costly recalls.

Case Studies in Quality Control

Manufacturing companies across various industries have adopted AI for quality control. For instance, BMW uses AI-powered image recognition to inspect vehicles for defects, ensuring high-quality standards. Coca-Cola employs AI to monitor the quality of its beverages, analysing factors such as colour, viscosity, and taste to ensure consistency.

Future Trends in AI Manufacturing

Increased Adoption of Collaborative Robots

Collaborative robots, or cobots, are designed to work alongside human workers, enhancing productivity and safety. AI enables these robots to perform complex tasks, adapt to changing environments, and collaborate seamlessly with humans. The adoption of cobots is expected to increase, driven by advancements in AI and robotics.

AI-Driven Supply Chain Optimization

AI will continue to optimise supply chains by enhancing demand forecasting, inventory management, and logistics. AI systems can analyse vast amounts of data to predict demand fluctuations, optimise stock levels, and improve delivery times, reducing costs and improving efficiency.

Enhanced Human-Machine Collaboration

The future of manufacturing will see greater collaboration between humans and machines, enabled by AI. Advanced AI systems will augment human capabilities, providing real-time insights, decision support, and automation of routine tasks. This collaboration will lead to increased productivity, innovation, and job satisfaction.

In conclusion, AI is transforming the manufacturing industry by enabling smart factories, predictive maintenance, and advanced quality control. As AI technology continues to evolve, it will drive further innovation and efficiency in manufacturing, creating new opportunities for growth and competitive advantage. Embracing AI in manufacturing is essential for companies looking to stay ahead in the rapidly changing industrial landscape.

Chapter 6: AI in Education

Personalised Learning

AI for Tailoring Educational Content to Individual Learners

AI revolutionises personalised learning by tailoring educational content to meet individual students' unique needs, preferences, and learning styles. AI algorithms analyse student performance, behaviour, and preferences data to create customised learning paths that adapt in real time. This ensures that each student receives the appropriate level of challenge and support, enhancing their learning experience and outcomes.

Tools and Platforms for Personalized Learning

Several tools and platforms leverage AI to deliver personalised learning experiences. Adaptive learning platforms, such as DreamBox and Knewton, adjust the difficulty and type of content based on a student's progress. Intelligent tutoring systems like Carnegie Learning offer personalised assistance, while personalised learning management systems (LMS) provide tailored content recommendations and learning activities.

Case Studies in Personalized Learning

Case studies demonstrate the effectiveness of AI-driven personalised learning. For example, Arizona State University implemented an AI-powered adaptive learning platform in its math courses, improving student performance and higher pass rates. Similarly, the Bridge International Academies in Kenya use AI to tailor educational content to students' needs, significantly enhancing learning outcomes in underserved communities.

Administrative Automation

AI for Streamlining Administrative Tasks in Educational Institutions

AI automates numerous administrative tasks in educational institutions, such as scheduling, grading, and admissions, freeing time for educators and administrators to focus on teaching and student support. AI systems handle repetitive tasks efficiently and accurately, increasing operational efficiency and reducing administrative burdens.

Examples of AI-Driven Administrative Automation

AI-powered chatbots can instantly manage student inquiries, responding to common questions about enrollment, courses, and campus services. Automated grading systems, like Gradescope, use AI to grade assignments and exams quickly and consistently. Predictive analytics tools help institutions manage enrollment, predict student retention, and optimise resource allocation.

Case Studies in Administrative Automation

Educational institutions worldwide have successfully adopted AI-driven administrative automation. For instance, Georgia State University uses predictive analytics to identify students at risk of dropping out and intervenes with targeted support, significantly improving retention rates. Similarly, Deakin University in Australia uses an AI-powered virtual assistant to handle student inquiries, enhancing the efficiency of their administrative processes.

Educational Content Creation

AI for Generating and Curating Educational Materials

AI assists in generating and curating high-quality educational materials, including textbooks, quizzes, and multimedia content. By analysing vast amounts of educational data, AI systems can identify key concepts and create content that aligns with curriculum standards and individual learning needs.

Techniques for AI-Based Educational Content Creation

Techniques for AI-based educational content creation include natural language processing (NLP), which helps AI understand and generate human language, and content recommendation systems, which suggest relevant materials based on a student's learning history. Automated content generation tools can create practice questions, generate summaries, and draft lesson plans.

Case Studies in Educational Content Creation

Several educational organisations have leveraged AI to create and curate educational materials. For example, Pearson uses AI to develop interactive learning materials that adapt to student progress. Quizlet employs AI to generate customised study sets based on user input, making study sessions more efficient and effective.

Future Trends in AI Education

Integration of Virtual Reality (VR) and AI

Integrating VR and AI promises to transform education by providing immersive and interactive learning experiences. AI can personalise VR environments to suit individual learning needs, making complex concepts easier to understand through visual and experiential learning.

AI-Driven Career Counseling

AI will enhance career counselling by analysing students' academic performance, interests, and market trends to provide personalised career advice. AI-driven platforms can match students with suitable career paths, recommend relevant courses, and connect them with job opportunities.

Enhanced Data Analytics for Educational Insights

AI will continue to improve data analytics in education, providing deeper insights into student performance, learning behaviours, and educational outcomes. These insights will help educators refine their teaching strategies, identify areas for improvement, and tailor interventions to support student success.

In conclusion, AI transforms education by enabling personalised learning, automating administrative tasks, and enhancing educational content creation. AI technology will offer new opportunities to improve academic outcomes, making learning more accessible, engaging, and effective. Embracing AI in education is essential for institutions seeking to provide high-quality, future-ready education to their students.

Chapter 7: Ethical Considerations and Future Trends

Ethical AI

Challenges and Considerations in Developing Ethical AI Systems

Developing ethical AI systems in education involves addressing biases, ensuring transparency, and maintaining accountability. If trained on biased data, AI models can unintentionally reinforce existing biases, leading to unfair outcomes. Therefore, it is crucial to implement measures that mitigate bias and promote fairness. Transparency in AI decision-making processes is also essential, as it helps build trust and allows for accountability.

Frameworks for Ensuring Fairness, Accountability, and Transparency

Frameworks such as the AI Ethics Guidelines and the AI Fairness 360 toolkit guide on creating ethical AI systems. These frameworks recommend best practices for data collection, algorithm development, and deployment to ensure AI systems are fair, transparent, and accountable. By following these guidelines, educational institutions can ensure that AI systems respect students' rights and promote equitable learning opportunities.

Regulatory Frameworks

Overview of AI Regulations and Standards

AI regulations and standards are evolving to address data privacy, security, and ethical use issues. Regulations such as the General Data Protection Regulation (GDPR) in Europe and the California Consumer Privacy Act (CCPA) in the United States set strict data handling and user consent guidelines. These regulations protect individuals' privacy and ensure that AI systems are used responsibly.

Global Perspectives on AI Governance

Countries have varying approaches to AI governance, reflecting their unique legal, cultural, and ethical considerations. For example, the European Union emphasises stringent data protection and ethical guidelines, while countries like China focus on rapid AI development, emphasising innovation and economic growth. Understanding these perspectives is essential for global AI deployment and compliance.

Future Trends in AI

Emerging Technologies and Their Potential Impact

Emerging technologies such as quantum computing, neuromorphic computing, and advanced robotics have the potential to revolutionise AI and its applications in education. Quantum computing could solve complex problems faster than classical computers, enhancing AI's capabilities. Neuromorphic computing aims to mimic the human brain's architecture, potentially leading to more efficient and robust AI systems. Advanced robotics can provide personalised and interactive learning experiences, enhancing educational outcomes.

Predictions for the Future of AI in Business and Society

AI will continue to transform industries, creating new opportunities and challenges. AI will enable more personalised and efficient learning experiences in education, improve administrative processes, and enhance educational content creation. Businesses will leverage AI to optimise operations, drive innovation, and gain a competitive edge. Society must adapt to these changes, address ethical considerations, and ensure that AI benefits everyone.

Conclusion

Recap of AI's Impact

AI has profoundly impacted various industries, driving efficiency, innovation, and competitive advantage. Its transformative potential continues to grow as new technologies and applications emerge.

Summary of Key Points from Each Chapter

A summary of key points from each chapter highlights AI's transformative potential across different sectors, showcasing the diverse applications and benefits of AI.

Overall Benefits of AI in Transforming Industries

AI's benefits include improved operational efficiency, enhanced decision-making, and the creation of new business opportunities. It enables businesses to innovate, adapt, and grow in a rapidly changing landscape.

Future Outlook

Anticipated Advancements in AI Technology

Advancements in AI technology will continue to drive innovation, offering new solutions to complex problems. Future developments in AI will enhance its capabilities and expand its applications.

Potential Challenges and Opportunities

AI presents challenges such as ethical considerations and regulatory compliance but also offers opportunities for businesses to innovate and grow. Addressing these challenges is crucial for maximising AI's benefits.

Call to Action for Businesses to Adopt AI

Encouragement for Businesses to Embrace AI
Businesses are encouraged to embrace AI to stay competitive and drive growth. Adopting AI technologies can significantly improve efficiency, innovation, and customer satisfaction.

Practical Steps for Integrating AI into Business Strategies
Practical steps include investing in AI research and development, partnering with AI experts, and adopting AI-driven solutions. Businesses should start small, pilot AI projects, and scale successful initiatives.

Encouragement and Inspiration

AI is not just a technology of the future; it is a powerful tool available today. Understanding and leveraging AI can unlock immense potential and transform your business, creating unprecedented growth and wealth opportunities. Embrace the future with confidence and become a leader in the AI-driven world.

In conclusion, as AI evolves, it will offer new opportunities for education, business, and society. By addressing ethical considerations, adhering to regulatory frameworks, and embracing emerging technologies, we can ensure that AI's transformative potential is realised in a way that benefits everyone.